BY ADRIENNE RICH

What Is Found There: Notebooks on Poetry and Politics
The Fact of a Doorframe: Poems 1950–2000
Fox: Poems 1998–2000
Arts of the Possible: Essays and Conversations
Midnight Salvage: Poems 1995–1998
Dark Fields of the Republic: Poems 1991–1995
Collected Early Poems 1950–1970
An Atlas of the Difficult World: Poems 1988–1991
Time's Power: Poems 1985–1988
Blood, Bread, and Poetry: Selected Prose, 1979–1985
Your Native Land, Your Life: Poems
Sources
A Wild Patience Has Taken Taken Me This Far: Poems 1978–1981
On Lies, Secrets, and Silence: Selected Prose, 1966–1978
The Dream of a Common Language: Poems 1974–1977
Twenty-one Love Poems
Of Woman Born: Motherhood as Experience and Institution
Poems: Selected and New, 1950–1974
Diving into the Wreck: Poems 1971–1972
The Will to Change
Leaflets
Necessities of Life
Snapshots of a Daughter-in-Law
The Diamond Cutters
A Change of World

THE SCHOOL
AMONG
THE RUINS

ADRIENNE RICH

THE SCHOOL AMONG THE RUINS

POEMS

2000–2004

W · W · NORTON & COMPANY · NEW YORK · LONDON

For information about permission to reproduce selections from this book,
write to Permissions, W. W. Norton & Company, Inc.,
500 Fifth Avenue, New York, NY 10110

Manufacturing by The Courier Companies, Inc.
Book design by Antonina Krass
Production manager: Amanda Morrison

Library of Congress Cataloging-in-Publication Data

Rich, Adrienne Cecile.
The school among the ruins : poems, 2000–2004 / Adrienne Rich.—1st ed.
p. cm.
ISBN 0-393-05983-9 (hardcover)
I. Title.
PS3535.I233S36 2004
811'.54—dc22
2004008370

W. W. Norton & Company, Inc.
500 Fifth Avenue, New York, N.Y. 10110
www.wwnorton.com

W. W. Norton & Company Ltd.
Castle House, 75/76 Wells Street, London W1t 3QT

1 2 3 4 5 6 7 8 9 0

FOR JEAN VALENTINE

CONTENTS

I

II
USONIAN JOURNALS 2000

III
TERRITORY SHARED

IV

ALTERNATING CURRENT

V

VI

DISLOCATIONS: SEVEN SCENARIOS

VII

VIII
TENDRIL

I

CENTAUR'S REQUIEM

Your hooves drawn together underbelly
shoulders in mud   your mane
of wisp and soil deporting all the horse of you

your longhaired neck
eyes   jaw yes   and ears
unforgivably human on such a creature
unforgivably what you are
deposited in the grit-kicked field of a champion

tender neck and nostrils   teacher   water-lily suction-spot
what you were   marvelous   we could not stand

Night drops   an awaited storm
driving in to wreck your path
Foam on your hide like flowers
where you fell   or fall   desire

2001

EQUINOX

Time split like a fruit between dark and light
and a usual fog drags
over this landfall
I've walked September end to end
barefoot room to room
carrying in hand a knife well honed for cutting stem or root
                              or wick   eyes open
to abalone shells   memorial candle flames
split lemons   roses laid
                    along charring logs   Gorgeous things
: : dull acres of developed land as we had named it: Nowhere
wetland   burnt garbage looming at its heart
gunmetal thicket   midnightblue blood and
                         tricking masks   I thought I knew
history was not a novel

So can I say it was not I   listed as Innocence
betrayed you   serving (and protesting always)
the motives of my government
thinking we'd scratch out a place
where poetry   old subversive shape
grew out of Nowhere   here?
where skin could lie on skin
a place "outside the limits"

                    Can say I was mistaken?

To be so bruised: in the soft organs   skeins of consciousness
Over and over have let it be
damage to others   crushing of the animate core
that tone-deaf cutloose ego swarming the world

so bruised: heart   spleen   long inflamed ribbons of the guts
the spine's vertical necklace swaying

Have let it swarm
through us   let it happen
as it must, inmost

but before this: long before this   those other eyes
frontally exposed themselves and spoke

2001

TELL ME

1

Tell me, why way toward dawn the body
close to a body familiar as itself
chills—tell me, is this the hour
                              remembered if outlived
as freezing—no, don't tell me

Dreams spiral birdwinged overhead
a peculiar hour   the silver mirror-frame's
quick laugh the caught light-lattice on the wall
as a truck drives off before dawn
headlights on

Not wanting
to *write this up*   for the public   not wanting
to *write it down*   in secret

just to lie here in this cold story
feeling it   trying to feel it through

2

Blink and smoke, flicking with absent nail
                                    at the mica bar
where she refills without asking
Crouch into your raingarb   this will be a night
unauthorized shock troops are abroad

this will be a night
the face-ghosts lean

over the banister
declaring the old stories all
froze like beards or frozen margaritas
all the new stories taste of lukewarm
margaritas, lukewarm kisses

3

From whence I draw this: *harrowed in defeats of language*
in history to my barest marrow
This: one syllable then another
gropes upward
one stroke laid on another
sound from one throat then another
never in the making
making beauty or sense

always mis-taken, draft, roughed-in
only to be struck out
is blurt is roughed-up
hot   keeps body
in leaden hour
simmering

2001

19

FOR JUNE, IN THE YEAR 2001

The world's quiver and shine
I'd clasp for you forever
jetty vanishing into pearlwhite mist
western sunstruck water-light

Touch food to the lips
let taste never betray you
cinnamon vanilla melting
on apple tart

but what you really craved:
a potency of words
Driving back from Berkeley
880's brute dystopia

I was at war with words
Later on C-Span: Tallahassee:
words straight to the point:
One person, one vote

No justice, no peace
it could lift you by the hair
it could move you like a wind
it could take you by surprise

as sudden Canada geese
took us by the marina
poised necks and alert
attitudes of pause

Almost home I wanted
you to smell the budding acacias
tangled with eucalyptus
on the road to Santa Cruz

2002

THE SCHOOL AMONG THE RUINS

Beirut. Baghdad. Sarajevo. Bethlehem. Kabul. Not of course here.

1

Teaching the first lesson and the last
—great falling light of summer will you last
longer than schooltime?
When children flow
in columns at the doors
BOYS GIRLS and the busy teachers

open or close high windows
with hooked poles   drawing darkgreen shades

closets unlocked, locked
questions unasked, asked, when

love of the fresh impeccable
sharp-pencilled   yes
order without cruelty

a street on earth   neither heaven nor hell
busy with commerce and worship
young teachers walking to school

fresh bread and early-open foodstalls

2

When the offensive rocks the sky when nightglare
misconstrues day and night when lived-in

rooms from the upper city
tumble cratering lower streets

cornices of olden ornament   human debris
when fear vacuums out the streets

When the whole town flinches
blood on the undersole thickening to glass

Whoever crosses   hunched   knees bent   a contested zone
knows why she does this suicidal thing

School's now in session day and night
children sleep
in the classrooms   teachers rolled close

3

How the good teacher loved
his school   the students
the lunchroom with fresh sandwiches

lemonade and milk
the classroom   glass cages
of moss and turtles
teaching responsibility

A morning breaks without bread or fresh-poured milk
parents or lesson plans

diarrhea first question of the day
children shivering   it's September
Second question: where is my mother?

4

One: I don't know where your mother
is   Two: I don't know
why they are trying to hurt us
Three: or the latitude and longitude
of their hatred   Four: I don't know if we
hate them as much   I think there's more toilet paper
in the supply closet   I'm going to break it open

Today this is your lesson:
write as clearly as you can
your name   home street   and number
down on this page
No you can't go home yet
but you aren't lost
this is our school

I'm not sure what we'll eat
we'll look for healthy roots and greens
searching for water though the pipes are broken

5

There's a young cat sticking
her head through window bars
she's hungry like us
but can feed on mice
her bronze erupting fur
speaks of a life already wild

her golden eyes
don't give quarter   She'll teach us   Let's call her
Sister
when we get milk we'll give her some

6

I've told you, let's try to sleep in this funny camp
All night pitiless pilotless things go shrieking
above us to somewhere

Don't let your faces turn to stone
Don't stop asking me why
Let's pay attention to our cat   she needs us

Maybe tomorrow the bakers can fix their ovens

7

"We sang them to naps   told stories   made
shadow-animals with our hands

wiped human debris off boots and coats
sat learning by heart the names
some were too young to write
some had forgotten how"

2001

THIS EVENING LET'S

not talk

about my country   How
I'm from an optimistic culture

that speaks louder than my passport
Don't double-agent-contra my

invincible innocence   I've
got my own

suspicions   Let's
order retsina

cracked olives and bread
I've got questions of my own but

let's give a little
let's let a little be

If *friendship is not a tragedy*
if it's a mercy

we can be merciful
if it's just escape

we're neither of us running
why otherwise be here

Too many reasons not
to waste a rainy evening

in a backroom of bouzouki
and kitchen Greek

I've got questions of my own but
let's let it be a little

There's a beat in my head
song of my country

called Happiness, U.S.A.
Drowns out bouzouki

drowns out world and fusion
with its *Get—get—get*

into your happiness before
happiness pulls away

hangs a left along the piney shore
weaves a hand at you—"one I adore"—

Don't be proud, run hard for that
enchantment boat

tear up the shore if you must but
get into your happiness because

before
and otherwise
it's going to pull away

So tell me later
what I know already

and what I don't get
yet   save for another day

Tell me this time
what you are going through

travelling the Metropolitan
Express

break out of that style
give me your smile
awhile

2001

VARIATIONS ON LINES FROM A CANADIAN POET

I need a gloss for the silence implicit in my legacy
for phantom Liberty standing bridal at my harbor
I need a gauze to slow the hemorrhaging of my history
I need an ancestor complicit in my undercover prying

I need soil that whirls and spirals upward somewhere else
I need dustbowl, sand dune, dustdevils for roots
I need the border-crossing eye of a tornado
I need an ancestor fleeing into Canada

to rampage freedom there or keep on fleeing
to keep on fleeing or invent a genre
to distemper ideology

2002

DELIVERED CLEAN

You've got to separate what they signify from what
they are   distinguish
their claimed intentions from the stuff coming
out from their hands and heads   The professor of cultural dynamics
taught us this   They're disasters   in absentia
really   when supposedly working
Look at the record:
lost their minds wrote bad checks and smoked in bed
and if they were men were bad with women and if they were women
picked men like that or would go with women
and talked too much and burnt the toast and abused all
known substances   Anyone who says
they were generous to a fault putting change
in whoever's cup if they had it on them   always room for the friend
with no place to sleep   refused to make what they made
in the image of the going thing
cooked up stews that could keep you alive with
gizzards and onions and splashes of raw
red wine   were
loyal where they loved and wouldn't name names
should remember   said the professor of cultural
dynamics   what
messes they made

The building will be delivered vacant
of street actors   so-called artists in residence
fast-order cooks on minimum wage
who dreamed up a life where space was cheap
muralists doubling as rabble-rousers
cross-dressing pavement poets
delivered clean

of those who harbor feral cats illegals illicit ideas
selling their blood to buy old vinyls
living at night and sleeping by day
with huge green plants in their windows
and huge eyes painted on their doors.

[for Jack Foley]

2002

THE EYE

A balcony, violet shade on stucco   fruit in a plastic bowl on the iron
   raggedy legged table, grapes and sliced melon, saucers, a knife, wine
in a couple of thick short tumblers cream cheese once came in: our snack
   in the eye of the war   There are places where fruit is implausible, even
rest is implausible, places where wine if any should be poured into wounds
   but we're not yet there or it's not here yet   it's the war
not us, that moves, pauses and hurtles forward into the neck
   and groin of the city, the soft indefensible places but not here yet

Behind the balcony an apartment, papers, pillows, green vines still watered
   there are waterless places but not here yet, there's a bureau topped
                                        with marble
and combs and brushes on it, little tubes for lips and eyebrows, a dish
                                        of coins and keys
   there's a bed a desk a stove a cane rocker a bookcase civilization
cage with a skittery bird, there are birdless places but not
   here yet, this bird must creak and flutter in the name of all
uprooted orchards, limbless groves
   this bird standing for wings and song that here can't fly

Our bed quilted   wine poured   future uncertain   you'd think
   people like us would have it scanned and planned   tickets to somewhere
would be in the drawer   with all our education you'd think we'd
                                        have taken measures
   soon as ash started turning up on the edges of everything ash
in the leaves of books ash on the leaves of trees and in the veins of
                                        the passive
   innocent life we were leading calling it hope
you'd think that and we thought this   it's the war not us that's moving
   like shade on a balcony

2002

THERE IS NO ONE STORY AND ONE STORY ONLY

The engineer's story of hauling coal
to Davenport for the cement factory, sitting on the bluffs
between runs looking for whales, hauling concrete
back to Gilroy, he and his wife renewing vows
in the glass chapel in Arkansas after 25 years
The flight attendant's story murmured
to the flight steward in the dark galley
of her fifth-month loss of nerve
about carrying the baby she'd seen on the screen
The story of the forensic medical team's
small plane landing on an Alaska icefield
of the body in the bag they had to drag
over the ice like the whole life of that body
The story of the man driving
600 miles to be with a friend in another country   seeming
easy when leaving but afterward
writing in a letter difficult truths
Of the friend watching him leave remembering
the story of her body
with his once and the stories of their children
made with other people and how his mind went on
pressing hers like a body
There is the story of the mind's
temperature neither cold nor celibate
Ardent   The story of
not one thing only.

2002

II

USONIAN
JOURNALS
2000

USONIAN JOURNALS 2000

[*Usonian:* the term used by Frank Lloyd Wright for his prairie-inspired architecture. Here, *of the United States of North America.*]

Citizen/Alien/Night/Mare

A country I was born and lived in undergoes rapid and flagrant change. I return here as a stranger. In fact I've lived here all along. At a certain point I realized I was no longer connected along any continuous strand to the nature of the change. I can't find my passport. Nobody asks me to show it.

Day/Job/Mare

. . . to lunch with K., USonian but recently from a British university. Described as "our Marxist." Dark and pretty, already she's got half the department classified: *She's crazy . . . He's carrying the chip of race on his shoulder . . . she's here because* he *is, isn't she? . . . He's not likely to make it through . . .* Ask her about current Brit. labor scene; she talks about the influence of the industrial revolution on Victorian prose. My aim: get clear of this, find another day job.

As we left the dark publike restaurant the street—ordinary enough couple of blocks between a parking lot and an office complex—broke into spitting, popping sounds and sudden running. I held back against the wall, she beside me. Something happened then everything. A man's voice screamed, then whined: a police siren starting up seemed miles away but then right there. I didn't see any blood. We ran in different directions, she toward, I away from, the police.

Document Window

Could I just show what's happening. Not that shooting, civil disturbance, whatever it was. I'd like you to see how differently we're all moving, how the time allowed to let things become known grows shorter and shorter, how quickly things and people get replaced. How interchangeable it all could get to seem. *Could get to seem . . .* the kind of phrase we use now, avoiding the verb *to be. There's a sense in which,* we say, dismissing other senses.

Rimbaud called for the rational derangement of all the senses in the name of poetry. Marx: capitalism deranges all the senses save the sense of property.

Keeping my back against unimportant walls I moved out of range of the confusion, away from the protection of the police. Having seen nothing I could swear to I felt at peace with my default. I would, at least, not be engaged in some mess not my own.

This is what I mean though: how differently we move now, rapidly deciding what is and isn't ours. Indifferently.

Voices

Wreathed around the entrance to a shopping mall, a student dining hall, don't pause for a word, or to articulate an idea. What hangs a moment in the air is already dead: *That's history.*

The moment—Edwin Denby describes it—when a dancer, leaping, stands still in the air. Pause in conversation when time would stop, an idea hang suspended, then get taken up and carried on. (Then that other great style of conversation: everyone at once, each possessed with an idea.) This newer conversation: *I am here and talking, talking, here and talking* . . . Television the first great lesson: against silence. "I thought she'd never call and I went aaah! to my friend and she went give it a week, she'll call you all right and you did"—"And you went waowh! and I went, right, I went O.K., it's only I was clueless? so now can we grab something nearby, cause I'm due on in forty-five?"

A neighbor painting his garage yelling in cell phone from the driveway: voice that penetrates kitchen-window glass. "Fucking worst day of my fucking life, fucking wife left me for another man, both on coke and, you know? I don't CARE! thought it was only maryjane she was, do you KNOW the prison term for coke? Fucking dealer, leaves me for him because she's HOOKED and I'm supposed to CARE? Do they know what they'll GET?"

Private urgencies made public, not collective, speaker within a bubble. In the new restaurant: "Marty? Thought I'd never get through to you. We need to move quickly with SZ-02, there are hounds on the trail. Barney won't block you at all. Just give him what we talked about."

USonian speech. Men of the upwardly mobilizing class needing to sound boyish, an asset in all the newness of the new: upstart, startup, adventurist, pirate lad's nasal bravado in the male vocal cords. Voices of girls and women screeking to an excitable edge of brightness. In an excessively powerful country, grown women sound like girls without authority or experience. Male, female voices alike pitched fastforward commercial, one timbre, tempo, intonation.

Mirrors

Possible tones of the human voice, their own possible physical beauty—no recognition. The fish-eye lens bobbles faces back.

Bodies heavy with sad or enraged feminine or macho brooding mimic stand-up comics, celebrities; grimace, gesticulate. The nakedest generation of young USonians with little intuition of the human history of nakedness, luminous inventions of skin and musculature. Their surfaces needlepointed with conventionally outrageous emblems, what mirror to render justly their original beauty back to them?

You touched me in places so deep I wanted to ignore you.

Artworks (I)

Painting on a gallery wall: people dwelling on opposite sides of a pane of glass. None of their eyes exchanging looks. Yellow flashes off the rug in the room and from the orchard beyond. House of people whose eyes do not meet.

White people doing and seeing no evil.

(Photograph of family reunion, eyes on the wide-lens camera, unmeeting.) "In fact I've lived here all along."

That was them not us. We were at the time in the time of our displacement, being torn from a false integrity. We stared at the pictures in the gallery knowing they were not us, we were being driven further for something else and who knew how far and for how long and what we were to do.

Stranger

Isolation begins to form, moves in like fog on a clear afternoon. Arrives with the mail, leaves its messages on the phone machine. If you hadn't undergone this so often it could take you by surprise, but its rime-white structure is the simple blueprint of your displacement. You: who pride yourself on not giving in, keep discovering in dreams new rooms in an old house, drawing new plans: living with strangers, enough for all, wild tomato plants along the road, redness for hunger and thirst. (Unrest, too, in the house of dreams: the underworld lashing back.)

But this fog blanks echoes, blots reciprocal sounds. The padded cell of a moribund democracy, or just your individual case?

Artworks (II)

Early summer lunch with friends, talk rises: poetry, urban design and planning, film. Strands of interest and affection binding us differently around the table. If an uneasy political theme rears up—the meaning of a show of lynching photographs in New York, after Mapplethorpe's photos, of sociopathic evil inside the California prison industry—talk fades. Not a pause but: a suppression. No one is monitoring this conversation but us. We know the air is bad in here, maybe want not to push that knowledge, ask *what is to be done?* How to breathe? *What will suffice?* Draft new structures or simply be aware? If art is our only resistance, what does that make us? If we're collaborators, what's our offering to corruption—an aesthetic, anaesthetic, dye of silence, withdrawal, intellectual disgust?

This fade-out/suspension of conversation: a syndrome of the past decades? our companionate immune systems under siege, viral spread of social impotence producing social silence?

Imagine written language that walks away from human conversation. A written literature, back turned to oral traditions, estranged from music and body. So what might reanimate, rearticulate, becomes less and less available.

41

Incline

Dreamroad rising steeply uphill; David is driving. I see it turning into a perpendicular structure salvaged from a long metal billboard: we will have to traverse this at a ninety-degree angle, then at the top go over and down the other side. There are no exits. Around is the Mojave Desert: open space. D.'s car begins to lose momentum as the incline increases; he tries shifting into a lower gear and gunning the engine. There is no way off this incline now, we're forced into a situation we hadn't reckoned on—a road now become something that is no road, something designated as "commercial space." I suggest rolling (ourselves in) the car down the steep dusty shoulder into the desert below, and out. For both of us, the desert isn't vacancy or fear, it's life, a million forms of witness. The fake road, its cruel deception, is what we have to abandon.

Mission Statement

The Organization for the Abolition of Cruelty has an air deployment with bases on every continent and on obscurer tracts of land. Airstrips and hangars have been constructed to accommodate large and small aircraft for reconnoiter and rescue missions whether on polar ice or in desert or rainforest conditions. Many types of craft are of course deployed to urban clusters. The mission of the Organization is not to the First, Third, or any other World. It is directed toward the investigation and abrogation of cruelty in every direction, including present and future extraterrestrial locations.

It is obvious that the destruction of despair is still our most urgent task. In this regard, we employ paramilitary methods with great care and watchfulness.

The personnel dedicated to this new program are responsible to the mis-

*sion, not to any national body. We are apprised of all new technologies
as soon as available. Hence we have a unique fusion of policy and tech-
nology, unique in that its purpose is the abolition of cruelty.*

*Ours is the first project of its kind to be fully empowered through the
new paranational charters. In principle, it is now recognized that both
agents and objects of cruelty must be rescued and transformed, and that
they sometimes merge into each other.*

<u>*In response to your inquiry:*</u> *this is a complex operation. We have a wide
range of specializations and concerns. Some are especially calibrated
toward language*

> *because of its known and unknown powers
>   to bind and to dissociate*

> *because of its capacity
>   to ostracize the speechless*

> *because of its capacity
>   to nourish self-deception*

> *because of its capacity
>   for rebirth and subversion*

> *because of the history
>   of torture
>   against human speech*

2000–2002

III

TERRITORY
SHARED

ADDRESS

Orientation of the word toward its addressee has an extremely high signifi-
cance. In point of fact, word is a two-sided act. It is determined equally by
whose word it is and *for whom* it is meant. . . . Each and every word expresses
the "one" in relation to the "other." . . . A word is territory shared by both
addressor and addressee, by the speaker and his interlocutor.

    —V. N. Voloshinov, *Marxism and the Philosophy of Language*

If all we would speak is ideology
believable walking past pent-up Christmas trees
in a California parking lot   day before Thanksgiving   hot sun
                                  on faint
scent of spruce   in the supermarket
mixed metaphors of food
faces expectant, baffled, bitter, distracted
wandering aisles or like me and the man ahead of me buying
                                  only milk
my car door grabbed open by a woman
thinking it her husband's car honking for her somewhere else

—and I think it true indeed I know
I who came only for milk am speaking it   :   though
would stand somewhere beyond
this civic nausea

: desiring not to stand apart
like Jeffers giving up on his kind   loving only unhuman creatures
because they transcend ideology   in eternity as he thought
but he wasn't writing to them
nor today's gull perched on the traffic light

Nor can this be about remorse
staring over its shopping cart

feeling its vague ideological thoughts

nor about lines of credit
blanketing shame and fear

nor being conscripted for violence
from without   beckoning at rage within

I know what it cannot be

But who   at the checkout this one day
do I address   who is addressing me
what's the approach whose the manners
whose dignity whose truth
when the change purse is tipped into the palm
for an exact amount without which

2002

TRANSPARENCIES

That the meek word like the righteous word can bully
that an Israeli soldier interviewed years
after the first Intifada could mourn on camera
what under orders he did, saw done, did not refuse
that another leaving Beit Jala could scrawl
on a wall: *We are truely sorry for the mess we made*
is merely routine   word that would cancel deed
That human equals innocent and guilty
That we grasp for innocence whether or no
is elementary   That words can translate into broken bones
That the power to hurl words is a weapon
That the body can be a weapon
any child on playground knows   That asked your favorite word
                                        in a game
you always named a thing, a quality, *freedom* or *river*
(never a pronoun never *God* or *War*)
is taken for granted   That word and body
are all we have to lay on the line
That words are windowpanes in a ransacked hut, smeared
by time's dirty rains, we might argue
likewise that words are clear as glass till the sun strikes it blinding

But that in a dark windowpane you have seen your face
That when you wipe your glasses the text grows clearer
That the sound of crunching glass comes at the height of the
                                        wedding
That I can look through glass
into my neighbor's house
but not my neighbor's life
That glass is sometimes broken to save lives

That a word can be crushed like a goblet underfoot
is only what it seems, part question, part answer: how
you live it

2002

LIVRESQUE

There hangs a space between the man
and his words

    like the space around a few snowflakes
    just languidly beginning

    space
    where an oil rig has dissolved in fog

man in self-arrest
between word and act

writing *agape, agape*
with a silver fountain pen

2002

COLLABORATIONS

I

Thought of this "our" nation :: thought of war
                                        ghosts of war fugitive
        in labyrinths of amnesia
veterans   out-of-date textbooks in a library basement
evidence trundled off   plutonium   under tarps after dark
        didn't realize it until I wrote it

August now   apples have started
                                        severing from the tree
over the deck   by night their dim impact
                                        thuds into dreams
by daylight bruised   starting to stew in sun
saying "apple" to nose and tongue
                                to memory
        Word following sense, the way it should be
and if you don't speak the word
                                do you lose your senses
And isn't this just one speck, one atom
                        on the glazed surface we call
America
        from which I write
                the war ghosts treading in their shredded
                                        disguises above the clouds
and the price we pay here still opaque as the fog
these mornings
                we always say will break open?

II

Try this on your tongue: "the poetry of the enemy"
If you read it will you succumb

Will the enemy's wren fly through your window
and circle your room

Will you smell the herbs hung to dry in the house
he has had to rebuild in words

Would it weaken your will to hear
riffs of the instruments he loves

rustling of rivers remembered
where faucets are dry

"The enemy's water"   is there a phrase
for that in your language?

And you   what do you write
now in your borrowed house   tuned in

to the broadcasts of horror
under a sagging arbor, *dimdumim*

do you grope for poetry
to embrace all this

—not describe, embrace   staggering
in its arms, Jacob-and-angel-wise?

III

Do you understand why I want your voice?
At the seder table it's said

you reclined and said nothing
now in the month of Elul is your throat so dry

your dreams so stony
you wake with their grit in your mouth?

There was a beautiful life here once
Our enemies poisoned it?

Make a list of what's lost but don't
call it a poem

that's for the scriptors of nostalgia
bent to their copying-desks

Make a list of what you love well
twist it   insert it

into a bottle of old Roman glass
go to the edge of the sea

at Haifa where the refugee ships lurched in
and the ships of deportation wrenched away

IV

for Giora Leshem

Drove upcoast   first day of another year   no rain
oxalis gold lakes floating
on January green

Can winter tides off the Levant
churn up wilder spume?

Think Crusades, remember Acre
wind driving at fortress walls

everything returns in time except the
utterly disappeared
What thou lovest well can well be reft from thee

What does not change / is the will
to vanquish
the fascination with what's easiest
see it in any video arcade

is this what the wind is driving at?

Where are you Giora?   whose hands
lay across mine a moment
Can you still believe that afternoon
talking   you smoking   light and shade
on the deck, here in California
our laughter, your questions of translation
your daughter's flute?

2002–2003

RITUAL ACTS

i

We are asking for books
No, not—but a list of books
to be given to young people
Well, to young poets
to guide them in their work
He gestures impatiently
They won't read he says
My time is precious
If they want to they'll find
whatever they need
I'm going for a walk after lunch
After that I lie down
Then and only then do I read the papers
Mornings are for work
the proofs of the second volume
—my trilogy, and he nods
And we too nod recognition

ii

The buses—packed
since the subways are forbidden
and the highways forsaken
so people bring everything on—
what they can't do without—
Air conditioners, sculpture
Double baskets of babies
Fruit platters, crematory urns
Sacks of laundry, of books
Inflated hearts, bass fiddles
Bridal gowns in plastic bags
Pet iguanas, oxygen tanks
The tablets of Moses

iii

After all—to have loved, wasn't that the object?
Love is the only thing in life
but then you can love too much
or the wrong way, you lose
yourself or you lose
the person
or you strangle each other
Maybe the object of love is
    to have loved
    greatly
    at one time or another
Like a cinema trailer
watched long ago

iv

You need to turn yourself around
face in another direction
She wrapped herself in a flag
soaked it in gasoline and lit a match
This is for the murdered babies
they say she said
Others heard
for the honor of my country
Others remember
the smell and how she screamed
Others say, This was just theater

v

This will not be a love scene
but an act between two humans
Now please let us see you
tenderly scoop his balls
into your hand
You will hold them
under your face
There will be tears on your face
That will be all
the director said
We will not see his face
He wants to do the scene
but not to show
his face

vi

A goat devouring a flowering plant
A child squeezing through a fence to school
A woman slicing an onion
A bare foot sticking out
A wash line tied to a torn-up tree
A dog's leg lifted at a standpipe
An old man kneeling to drink there
A hand on the remote

We would like to show but to not be obvious
except to the oblivious
We want to show ordinary life
We are dying to show it

2003

POINT IN TIME

If she's writing a letter on a sheet of mica
to be left on the shelf of the cave
with the century's other letters each
stained with its own DNA expressed
in love's naked dark or the dawn
of a day of stone:
it's a fact like a town crosshaired on a map
But we are not keeping archives here
where all can be blown away
nor raking the graves in Père-Lachaise
nor is she beholden or dutiful
as her pen pushes its final stroke
into the mineral page
molecule speaking to molecule
for just this moment

This is the point in time when
she must re-condense her purpose
like ink, like rain, like winter light
like foolishness and hatred
like the blood her hand first knew
as a wet patch on the staircase wall
she was feeling her way down in the dark.

2003

IV

ALTERNATING CURRENT

ALTERNATING CURRENT

Sometimes I'm back in that city
in its/   not my/   autumn
                    crossing a white bridge
over a dun-green river
eating shellfish with young poets
under the wrought-iron roof of the great market
drinking with the dead poet's friend
                    to music struck
from odd small instruments

walking arm in arm with the cinematographer
through the whitelight gardens of Villa Grimaldi
earth and air stretched
to splitting still
                    his question:
have you ever been in a place like this?

No bad dreams.   Night, the bed, the faint clockface.
No bad dreams.   Her arm or leg or hair.
No bad dreams.   A wheelchair unit screaming
off the block.   No bad dreams.   Pouches of blood: red cells,
plasma.   Not here.   No, none.   Not yet.

Take one, take two
—camera out of focus   delirium swims
across the lens   Don't get me wrong   I'm not
critiquing your direction
but I was there   saw what you didn't
take   the care
you didn't   first of yourself then
of the child   Don't get me wrong I'm on
your side but standing off
where it rains   not on the set where it's
not raining yet
take three

What's suffered in laughter   in aroused afternoons
in nightly yearlong back-to-back
wandering each others' nerves and pulses
O changing love that doesn't change

A deluxe blending machine
A chair with truth's coat of arms
A murderous code of manners
A silver cocktail reflecting a tiny severed hand
A small bird stuffed with print and roasted
A row of Lucite chessmen filled with shaving lotion
A bloodred valentine to power
A watered-silk innocence
A microwaved foie gras
A dry-ice carrier for conscience donations
A used set of satin sheets folded to go
A box at the opera of suffering
A fellowship at the villa, all expenses
A Caterpillar's tracks gashing the environment
A bad day for students of the environment
A breakdown of the blending machine
A rush to put it in order
A song in the chapel a speech a press release

As finally by wind or grass
     drive-ins
                    where romance always was
an after-dark phenomenon
                                   lie crazed and still
great panoramas lost to air
      this time this site of power shall pass
               and we remain or not but not remain
      as now we think we are

for J.J.

When we are shaken out

when we are shaken out to the last vestige
when history is done with us
   when our late grains glitter
                           salt swept into shadow
    indignant and importunate strife-fractured crystals
will it matter if our tenderness (our solidarity)
                     abides in residue
  long as there's tenderness and solidarity

Could the tempos and attunements of my voice
  in a poem or yours or yours and mine
in telephonic high hilarity
                  cresting above some stupefied inanity
   be more than personal

(and—as you once said—what's wrong with that?)

2002–2003

V

If some long unborn friend
looks at photos in pity,
we say, sure we were happy,
but it was not in the wind.

MEMORIZE THIS

i

Love for twenty-six years, you can't stop
A withered petunia's crisp   the bud sticky   both are dark
The flower engulfed in its own purple   So common, nothing
                                             like it
The old woodstove gone to the dump
Sun plunges through the new skylight
This morning's clouds piled like autumn in Massachusetts
This afternoon's far-flung like the Mojave
Night melts one body into another
One drives fast the other maps a route
Thought new it becomes familiar
From thirteen years back maybe
One oils the hinges one edges the knives
One loses an earring the other finds it
One says I'd rather make love
Than go to the Greek Festival
The other, I agree.

ii

Take a strand of your hair
on my fingers let it fall
across the pillow   lift to my nostrils
inhale your body entire

Sleeping with you after
weeks apart   how normal
yet   after midnight
to turn and slide my arm
along your thigh
drawn up in sleep
what delicate amaze

2002–2003

THE PAINTER'S HOUSE

Nineteen-thirties midwestern
—the painter long gone to the sea—
plutonic sycamore by the shed
a mailbox open mouthed
in garden loam a chip
of veiny china   turned
up there where he might have stood

eyeing the dim lip of grass
beyond, the spring stars sharpening
above

Well since there's still light   walk around
stand on the porch
cup hands around eyes peering in

Is this the kitchen where she worked and thought
Is that the loft where their bodies fell
into each other   The nail where the mirror
hung   the shelf where her college books
eyed her aslant
Those stairs would her bare feet have felt?

In the mute shed no trace
of masterworks   occult
fury of pigment   no
downslash of provocation
no whirled hands at the doorjamb
no lightning streak   no stab in the dark
no   sex   no   face

2003

AFTER APOLLINAIRE & BRASSENS

When the bridge of lovers bends
over the oilblack river
and we see our own endings
through eyes aching and blearing
when the assault begins
and we're thrown apart still longing

when the Bridge of Arts trembles
under the streaked sky
when words of the poets tumble
into the shuddering stream
where who knew what joy
would leap after what pain

what flows under the Seine
Mississippi Jordan Tigris
Elbe Amazon Indus Nile

and all the tributaries
who knows where song goes
now and from whom
toward what longings

2003

SLASHES

Years pass   and two   who once
don't know each other at all
dark strokes gouge a white wall   as lives
and customs slashed by dates :   October '17 / May '68
                                                           / September '73
Slash across lives   memory pursues its errands
   a lent linen shirt pulled unabashedly over her naked shoulders
      cardamom seed bitten in her teeth
                                                watching him chop onions
   words in the air   *segregation/partition/apartheid*
   vodka/cigarette smoke   a time
                                          vertigo on subway stairs
Years pass   she pressing the time into a box
not to be opened   a box
quelling pleasure and pain

You could describe something like this
in gossip   write a novel   get it wrong

   In wolf-tree, see the former field
The river's muscle :   greater than its length
the lake's light-blistered blue :   scorning
                circumference
A map inscribes relation
                            only when
underground aquifers are fathomed in
water table rising or falling
      beneath apparently
         imperturbable earth

   music from a basement session overheard

2002

TRACE ELEMENTS

Back to the shallow pond   sharp rotting scatter
leaf-skinned edge there   where the ring
couldn't be sunk far out enough
                         (far enough from shore)

back out the rock-toothed logging road
to the dark brook where it's dropped   mudsucked gold
                         (sucked under stones)
that's another marriage   lucid and decisive
to say at last: I did, I do, I will
                       (I did not, I will not)

   Snow-whirled streetlamps under a window
                       (a bedroom and a window)
   icy inch of the raised sash   blizzard clearing to calm
   outlined furniture: figured mirror: bedded bodies:
                warm blood: eyes in the dark:
                         no contradiction:
              She was there
   and they were there: her only   now   seeing it   (only now)

Bow season: then gun season
Apricot leaves bloodsprinkled: soaked: case closed

Memory: echo in time

All's widescreen now   lurid inchoate century
Vast disappearing acts   *the greatest show on earth*

but here are small clear refractions
from an unclear season

blood on a leaf
gold trace element in water
light from the eye behind the eye

2003

BRACT

Stories of three islands
you've told me, over years
over meals, after quarrels,
light changing the spectrum of your hair
your green eyes, lying on our backs
naked or clothed, driving
through wind, eighteen-wheeler trucks
of produce crates ahead and behind
you saying, I couldn't live long
far from the ocean

Spring of new and continuing
war, harpsichord crashing
under Verlet's fingers
I tell you I could not live long
far from your anger
lunar reefed and tidal
bloodred bract from spiked stem
tossing on the ocean

2003

VI

DISLOCATIONS:
SEVEN
SCENARIOS

DISLOCATIONS: SEVEN SCENARIOS

1

Still learning the word
"home" or what it could mean
                    say, to relinquish

  a backdrop of Japanese maples turning
  color of rusted wheelbarrow bottom
  where the dahlia tubers were thrown

You must go live in the city now
over the subway though not on
                    its grating

must endure the foreign music
of the block party

finger in useless anger
the dangling cords of the window blind

2

In a vast dystopic space the small things
multiply

when all the pills run out the pain
grows more general

flies find the many eyes
quarrels thicken then
                            weaken

tiny mandibles of rumor open and close
blame has a name that will not be spoken

you grasp or share a clot of food
according to your nature
                            or your strength

love's ferocity snarls
from under the drenched blanket's hood

3

City and world: this infection drinks like a drinker
whatever it can

casual salutations first
little rivulets of thought

then wanting stronger stuff
sucks at the marrow of selves

the nurse's long knowledge of wounds
the rabbi's scroll of ethics
the young worker's defiance

only the solipsist seems intact
in her prewar building

4

For recalcitrancy of attitude
the surgeon is transferred
to the V.A. hospital   where poverty
is the administrator
of necessity and her
orders don't necessarily
get obeyed
because
the government
is paying
and the
used-to-be
warriors
are patients

5

Faces in the mesh: defiance or disdain
    remember Paul Nizan?
        You thought you were innocent if you said

"I love this woman and I want to live
    in accordance with my love"
        but you were beginning the revolution

maybe so, maybe not
    look at her now
        pale lips papery flesh

at your creased belly   wrinkled sac
    look at the scars
        reality's autographs

along your ribs across her haunches
look at the collarbone's reverberant line

    how in a body can defiance
    still embrace its likeness

6

Not to get up and go back to the drafting table
where failure crouches accusing
like the math test you bluffed and flunked
so early on
not to drag into the window's
cruel and truthful light   your blunder
not to start over

but to turn your back, saying
all anyway is compromise
impotence and collusion
from here on I will be no part of it

is one way could you afford it

7

Tonight someone will sleep in a stripped apartment
the last domestic traces, cup and towel
awaiting final disposal

—has ironed his shirt for travel
left an envelope for the cleaning woman
on the counter under the iron

internationalist turning toward home
three continents to cross   documents declarations
searches queues

and home no simple matter
of hearth or harbor
bleeding from internal wounds

he diagnosed   physician
without frontiers

2002

VII

FIVE O'CLOCK, JANUARY 2003

Tonight as cargoes of my young
fellow countrymen and women are being hauled
into positions aimed at death, positions
they who did not will it suddenly
have to assume
I am thinking of Ed Azevedo
half-awake in recovery
if he has his arm whole
and how much pain he must bear
under the drugs
On cliffs above a beach
luxuriant in low tide after storms
littered with driftwood hurled and piled and
humanly arranged in fantastic
installations and beyond
silk-blue and onion-silver-skinned
Jeffers' "most glorious creature on earth"
we passed, greeting, I saw his arm
bandaged to the elbow
asked and he told me: It was just
a small cut, nothing, on the hand he'd
washed in peroxide thinking
that was it until the pain began
traveling up his arm
and then the antibiotics the splint the
numbing drugs the sick sensation
and this evening at five o'clock the emergency
surgery and last summer
the train from Czechoslovakia to Spain
with his girl, cheap wine, bread and cheese
room with a balcony, ocean like this

nobody asking for pay in advance
kindness of foreigners
in that country, sick sensation now
needing to sit in his brother's truck again
even the accident on the motorcycle
was nothing like this
I'll be thinking of you at five
this evening I said
afterward you'll feel better, your body
will be clean of this poison
I didn't say Your war is here
but could you have believed
that from a small thing infection
would crawl through the blood
and the enormous ruffled shine
of an ocean wouldn't tell you.

2003

WAIT

In paradise every
the desert wind is rising
third thought
in hell there are no thoughts
is of earth
sand screams against your government
issued tent   hell's noise
in your nostrils   crawl
into your ear-shell
wrap yourself in no-thought
wait   no place for the little lyric
wedding-ring glint the reason why
on earth
they never told you

2003

DON'T TAKE ME

too seriously   please
   take the December goodness
      of my neighbors' light-strung eaves
   take the struggle helping with the tree
      for the children's sake
         don't take me seriously
   on questionnaires about faith and fault
      and country   Don't
         take me for a loner don't take me for a foreigner don't
   take me in the public
         library checking definitions
            of freedom in the dictionary or
   tracing satellites after curfew
or in my Goodwill truck delivering a repaired TV
   to the house of the foil'd revolutionary

2002

TO HAVE WRITTEN THE TRUTH

To have spent hours stalking the whine of an insect
have smashed its body in blood on a door
then lain sleepless with rage

to have played in the ship's orchestra crossing
the triangle route
dissonant arpeggios under cocktail clatter

to have written the truth in a lightning flash
then crushed those words in your hand
balled-up and smoking

when self-absolution
easygoing pal of youth
leans in the doorframe

Kid, you always
        took yourself so hard!

2003

SCREEN DOOR

Metallic slam on a moonless night
A short visit and so we departed.
A short year with many long
                                days
A long phone call with many   pauses.
                        It was gesture's code
we were used to using, we were
                                awkward without it.

Over the phone: knocking heard
at a door in another country.
Here it's tonight: there tomorrow.
A vast world we used to think small.
That we knew everyone who mattered.

Firefly flicker.   Metallic slam.   A moonless night.   Too dark
                                for gesture.
But it was gesture's code we were used to.
                                Might need again.   Urgent
                                hold-off or beckon.

Fierce supplication. One finger pointing: "Thither."
Palms flung upward: "What now?"
Hand slicing the air or across the throat.
A long wave to the departing.

2003

VIII

TENDRIL

TENDRIL

1

Why does the outstretched finger of home
probe the dark hotel room like a flashlight beam

on the traveller, half-packed, sitting on the bed
face in hands, wishing her bag emptied again at home

Why does the young security guard
pray to keep standing watch forever, never to fly

Why does he wish he were boarding
as the passengers file past him into the plane

What are they carrying in their bundles
what vanities, superstitions, little talismans

What have the authorities intercepted
who will get to keep it

2

Half-asleep in the dimmed cabin
she configures a gecko

aslant the overhead bin   tendrils of vine
curling up through the cabin floor

buried here in night as in a valley
remote from rescue

Unfound, confounded, vain, superstitious, whatever we were
                                        before
now we are still, outstretched, curled, however we were

Unwatched the gecko, the inching of green
through the cracks in the fused imperious shell

3

Dreaming a womb's languor valleyed in death
among fellow strangers

she has merely slept through the night
a nose nearby rasps, everyone in fact is breathing

the gecko has dashed into some crevice
of her brain, the tendrils retract

orange juice is passed on trays
declarations filled out in the sudden dawn

4

She can't go on dreaming of mass death
this was not to have been her métier

she says to the mirror in the toilet
a bad light any way you judge yourself

and she's judge, prosecutor, witness, perpetrator
of her time

's conspiracies of the ignorant
with the ruthless   She's the one she's looking at

5

This confessional reeks of sweet antiseptic
and besides she's not confessing

her mind balks   craving wild onions
nostril-chill of eucalyptus

that seventh sense of what's missing
against what's supplied

She walks at thirty thousand feet into the cabin
sunrise crashing through the windows

Cut the harping she tells herself
You're human, porous like all the rest

6

She was to have sat in a vaulted
library   heavy scrolls wheeled to a desk

for sieving, sifting, translating
all morning   then a quick lunch   thick coffee

then light descending slowly
on earthen-colored texts

but that's a dream of dust
frail are thy tents   humanity

facing thy monologues of force
She must have fallen asleep reading

7

She must have fallen asleep reading
The woman who mopped the tiles

is deliquescent   a scarlet gel
her ligaments and lungs

her wrought brain   her belly's pulse
disrupt among others mangled there

the chief librarian the beggar
the man with the list of questions

the scrolls never to be translated
and the man who wheeled the scrolls

8

She had wanted to find meaning in the past but the future drove
a vagrant tank a rogue bulldozer

rearranging the past in a blip
coherence smashed into vestige

not for her even the thought
of her children's children picking up

one shard of tile then another laying
blue against green seeing words

in three scripts flowing through vines and flowers
guessing at what it was

the levantine debris
Not for her but still for someone?

2003

NOTES ON THE POEMS

Tell Me

remembered if outlived / as freezing: Emily Dickinson, *The Complete Poems,* ed. Thomas H. Johnson (Boston: Little, Brown, 1960), no. 341.

harrowed in defeats of language: Michael Heller, "Sag Harbor, Whitman, As If An Ode," in *Wordflow: New and Selected Poems* (Jersey City, N.J.: Talisman House, 1997), p. 129.

in history to my barest marrow: Black Salt: Poems by Édouard Glissant, trans. Betsy Wing (Ann Arbor: University of Michigan Press, 1998), p. 33.

This evening let's

friendship is not a tragedy: See June Jordan, "Civil Wars" (1980), in *Some of Us Did Not Die: New and Selected Essays* (New York: Basic Books, 2002), p. 267.

Delivered Clean

"Delivered vacant" is a developer's phrase for a building for sale whose tenants have already been evicted. See Rebecca Solnit, *Hollow City: The Siege of San Francisco and the Crisis of American Urbanism* (New York: Verso, 2000), p. 158.

Transparencies

we are truely sorry . . . Clyde Haberman, "Palestinians Reclaim Their Town after Israelis Withdraw," *New York Times,* August 31, 2001, p. A6.

Collaborations

dimdumim: Hebrew for "dawn," "dusk," "twilight."

what thou lovest well . . . See Ezra Pound, *The Pisan Cantos* (London: Faber & Faber, 1959), p. 112: "what thou lovest well remains . . . cannot be reft from thee."

what does not change . . . See Charles Olson, "The Kingfishers," in his *Selected Poems* (Berkeley: University of California Press, 1997), p. 5: "What does not change / is the will to change."

the fascination with what's easiest . . . See W. B. Yeats, "The Fascination of What's Difficult," in his *Collected Poems*, 2nd ed. (New York: Macmillan, 1950), p. 104.

Alternating Current

The Villa Grimaldi outside Santiago, formerly a military officers' club, was converted to a detention and torture facility during the Pinochet regime in Chile. It is now a memorial park honoring the victims of torture.

V

If some long unborn friend . . . : Muriel Rukeyser, "Tree of Days," in *Muriel Rukeyser, Selected Poems*, ed. Adrienne Rich (New York: Library of America, 2004), p. 69.

After Apollinaire & Brassens

Derived from Guillaume Apollinaire's poem "Le Pont Mirabeau" and Georges Brassens's song "Le Pont des Arts."

Slashes

October '17 / May '68 / September '73: October 1917 marked the beginning of the Bolshevik Revolution in Russia, a determinative event in twentieth-century history. May 1968 saw massive popular U.S. opposition to the war in Vietnam, linked with the movement for Black civil rights and with anticolonial struggles abroad; in France there were uprisings of workers and students. On September 11, 1973, in Chile, a military coup under General Augusto Pinochet backed by the CIA violently seized power from the elected socialist government of Salvador Allende.

In wolf-tree, see the former field: See Anne Whiston Spirn, *The Language of Landscape* (New Haven: Yale University Press, 1998), pp. 18–19: "A 'wolf' tree is a tree within a woods, its size and form, large trunk and horizontal branches, anomalous to the environs of slim-trunked trees with upright branches . . . a clue to the open field in which it once grew alone, branches reaching laterally to the light and up."

Dislocations: Seven Scenarios—5

You thought you were innocent . . . See Paul Nizan, *Aden Arabie* (New York: Monthly Review Press, 1968), p. 131.

Five O'Clock, January 2003

most glorious creature on earth: See Robinson Jeffers, "Ninth Anniversary," in *The Wild God of the World: An Anthology of Robinson Jeffers,* ed. Albert Gelpi (Stanford, Calif.: Stanford University Press, 2003), p. 52: "there the most glorious / Creature on earth shines in the nights or glitters in the suns, / Or feels of its stone in the blind fog."

ACKNOWLEDGMENTS

Thanks to the following publications in which some of these poems have appeared, sometimes in earlier versions:

American Poetry Review

Bloom: Queer Fiction, Art, Poetry and More

Boston Review

Brick (Toronto)

Bridges: A Journal for Jewish Feminists and Our Friends

Connect: Art Politics Theory Practice

Hunger

Logos: A Journal of Modern Society and Culture (www.logosjournal.com)

Long Shot

Massachusetts Review

Michigan Quarterly Review

Monthly Review: An Independent Socialist Magazine

Poets Against the War (Nation Books, Sam Hamill, editor)

Present Tense: Poets in the World
(Mark Pawlak and Ron Schreiber, editors; Hanging Loose Press)

The Progressive

Seattle Journal for Social Justice

Tri-Quarterly, a publication of Northwestern University

Water-Stone

XCP: Cross-Cultural Poetics

ZYZZYVA